QUEEN SURVIVED

An inspirational POETRY book
written by

QUEEN AMINA

The Dedication

This book is for all the ones that never gave up on me in my journey. The loyal ones that always and forever believed in the Queen and knew that I would once again rise to my fullest sunshinest QueenAmina ever. The true ones beyond a shadow of a doubt had my back to the fullest... this one's for you!!

I love and appreciate you all

LOVE QUEEN AMINA

FIRST POEM

In the midst of my pain
About to go insane
God brought me, you!
The light shining through
In the time of need
I got on my knees to plead
And God brought me you
To happily say " I do"
In the midst of my hurt
God brought you to flirt
With my soul
Right before my heart turned cold
He gave me to you
To love you eternally through and through
In the midst of giving up
Not giving one fuck
God brought me, you!
To love totally true
He gave us each other
To be much more than a lover
To be my strength when I am weak
To be totally faithful and never cheat
To be loyal as can be
To see what the others could not see
When I was totally done
God said here daughter this is the one
God brought me, you!
A part of me so true
God brought you your rib
That's what he did
He gave me
What I didn't see
Unconditional Love
That how I know it's from God above
When I am about to jump to my end
God said here is your other half now let your
real journey begin
When I was on the edge of my seat
He gave me back my heartbeat

The more my soul grew
God brought me, you!
What I am saying is I will love you from here to the moon
And I am praying to be in your arms soon
When I was in tears
You washed away my fears
When I think of us
It starts with trust
So... understand this, my man
I will do all that I can
To listen and comprehend
Your plan
The fact is that I look forward to our life together
Happiness in every weather
You are not just a lover but a true friend
With you, all our pain will end
I will always give you my heart
I pray that everyday is like our start
God brought me, you!
When I thought my days were few
I ask God
To push the devil aside
So that we can enjoy this ride
Your last name I will carry with pride
You are embedded in my soul
I want to make you happy until I am grey and old
I look into your eyes
And to my surprise
I see me in you
One more reason I can't wait to say "I Do"
I have butterflies in my tummy when it comes to you
I will always be loyal and true
With our energy shining through
God brought me, you!
You are my light
For you, I will always keep it tight
You are my air and everything
I am totally yours with or without a ring
That fact that I am in love with you
Guarantees that I will always be true.

love ♥

SECOND POEM

Sometimes when I'm about to be in tears
You wipe away my fears
When I feel like I am not good enough
You show me that my past was tough
But my future will be more
Because of everything I had to endure
You show me that I too can be adored
And never let my past keep me floored
I do
need you to know
That you are a want and a need
And because of you my heart can be freed
You make me see happiness
You make me feel that life with
you will be pure bliss
You opened my spirit and my heart
And daddy please know till death do us part!!!

Bliss

Happiness

Heart

THIRD POEM

Open your eyes and rise!!!!
I haven't posted a poem in some time
Keeping my talent to myself is a real crime
My heart said let it flow
My body said don't forget to stop the show
The two got together
And even in this cold weather
They decided to make a point
They wanted to get loose in this joint
You know how it goes
When you have a tingle in your head all the way down to your toes
It started in my mind
Then made it's way down to my spine
God was shining on me so I know it's a blessing
For me to teach you all a lesson
For me to tell you all

What's written all over my wall

Teach you all how to treat each other

Teach you all to be faithful to just one lover

Teach you all to always be true inside

Teach you all how to swallow your pride

Help you all through the storm

Help you all learn how to stay warm

Help you all figure out your mission

Help you all get through this crazy transition

Ask you all to love one another

Ask you all to honor thy mother

Ask you men to stand up and be a father

sk you to take good care of your children and know that they are a blessing and NOT a bother

My heart told me to let this flow

My soul said to stand up and never let it go

My spirit told me it's time for us all to grow

My mind said to lead by example and always let your truth show

It's time for all people to unite

We all know it's going to be a long fight

However it's one that we need to win

Or our world will be overcome with death and sin

So I will ask you all one finally question

Have you picked up any of this lesson

Do you hear my message loud and clear

I am asking people everywhere

Do you know

What you need to show

Or how much you all need to grow

If so!

Stand with me united for change

And tell everyone in ear range

That we must stand together

No matter what the weather

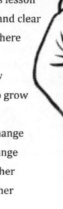

FOURTH POEM

I want to feel you close to me
I want total intimacy
I don't want sex you can get that anywhere
I want a connection only we can hear
Only we can smell or feel
That is undoubtedly real
I want to be so close that I feel your heartbeat
I want to intertwine our bodies down to our feet
Have our toes rubbing
While we're intently hugging
Inhaling your exhale
Getting high from your smell
Body sensitive all over
As you run your fingers down my shoulder
Giving me goosebumps
Kissing on my lady lumps
Hold me in your hands
Squeezing me as only you can
Me...
Uncontrollably
Allowing my juices to flow
Close enough to feel your manhood grow
The emotions are too real not wanting the feeling to stop
Moving so passionately not knowing who's on top
Running your fingers down my spine
Whispering in my ear "You're Mine"
Nipples hard, pussy wet
Dick as hard as it could get
But no penetrating
Mind racing
Emotions chasing
Spirits phasing
In your eyes, I'm gazing
As your lips touch mine... simply amazing

Moaning as your fingers tickle my skin
Wanting you deep within
My mental
So sensual
Tasting you on my lips
Grinding my hips
My pussy drips
With every forceful grip
Wanting you so much
Enhancing with every touch
Passionately inter-tangled
Our bodies mingled
Intimately
Mentally
Having that connection from the start
Comes from the heart
The mind and the soul
Not to be so bold

FOURTH POEM

But will you take this journey
With me
To ecstasy
Learning each other for eternity
Having orgasms
Without sex
Rubbing you down instead of getting you vexed
Being freaks for each other
Mental lovers
Can you understand the intimacy
Of being with me
I want to play with myself in front of you
Just to see what you would do....
I want to give you head every chance I get
Just to show you that "I'm it"
I want to make you smile every day
Just to show you that I think of you that way
I want to be your strength and your pain
Just to show you that love is insane
Can't wait until the morning that I wake up wrapped in your arms
Knowing that I'm totally safe from harm
Inhaling your every breathe
Happily with my head on your chest
Listening to your heartbeat
As it slowly puts me to sleep

FIFTH POEM

Quietly I sit alone
Comfortable in my skin because I am grown
Learning more
So mature
Looking deep within myself
Don't need any help
growing
I'm glowing
My soul
is as pure as gold

I am a diamond in the rough
The outside shell is very tough
It's never easy to get to the good inside
learning me is no easy ride
building me was a wonderful stride
I'm full of pride
I know how hard I tried
So strong I think I never cried
So I sit alone
mind free to roam
heart has never been owned
It's okay because I am grown
sitting silently
engaged in me
sexier than anyone can be
spirit is so free

However, I ask myself
I'm in good health
so why am I alone
No one on my phone
am I not amazingly wonderful
does anyone know just how cool
I truly am inside
this is why I hide
because people want my body
because I am a hottie
I want someone who wants my mind
not my behind
I want someone to be my equal
I'm the only me you get no sequel
So I will just sit here and continue to grow
because I personally know
I am happy with me
and the true reality
of it all
is I stand proud and tall
comfortable in my skin
because I so love the me within!

I wish I could take it all back

I wish you were a myth and NOT Fact

I wish I could trust

I swear it's a must

I need to live free

Please God just let me be

Give me my peace of mind

I want this pain to be left behind

What makes you stand on the edge

One step from the ledge

I just can't with the hurt and pain

I swear it is driving me insane

I was peaceful and good

Doing everything I should

Help me God I am on my knees

Begging, please

Save me from my past

To ensure my future will last

God bless me as only you can

Because I swear I found the perfect man

God, please heal my heart

I feel that we should never part

God I ask that you wipe my slate clean

Because for this man I am a fiend

I wish that I could rise above

Because I swear I am in love.....

I will end this in a prayer

That God will take away all my fear

Let me walk in my faith

To keep this progressing at a positive pace

Moving upward toward all our goal

Because I swear this man is to have and to hold

Amen!!

Now let our future begin!!!

SIXTH POEM

SEVENTH POEM

Why did it take so long?
Did God want to know if I was strong?
Was God aware I sang my last love song
Did God know that everything was going wrong?
DAMN! everything my heart went through
It was all worth it to end up with you
The pain and heartache
So surprised that my spirit did not break
The suffering I had to endure
Did God want to watch me mature?

The cheating

My life depleting

The lying

Me on my knees crying

Sick of trying

The questions, ex's called it prying

The late nights

All the street fights

Always feeling anger at their sight

Wishing I was a bird that could take flight

Feeling sick

while they run around slinging dick

all the fucking cheating they did

I should have known I was dealing with a kid

Sometimes we are blinded

however, a relationship should not be undermined

I just want to truly "Thank God" for building me

To ensure that I could finally see

The blessings

The learned lessons

The things to not accept

Forgiving but never to forget

On my knees saying Thank you

for allowing me to push through

for making me strong

for showing me everything that was wrong

for making sure that I healed inside and out

for bringing me "TRUE LOVE" without a doubt

For bringing me a Real King

That got down on his knee with a ring

That will never cheat or lie

SEVENTH POEM

That never wants to see a tear fall from my eye

That makes me smile every chance he can

for finally blessing me with a real man

That wants to build

That wants to be my shield

That lives with the intent to make me shine

That I am his and he is all mine

A man that knows and respects the Queen

A man that is real but makes everything feel like a dream

A true warrior here to help lead

They will keep you on a pedestal

they will be an extension of you

and they will be all in for saying "I DO"

They will always show you what you mean

always making you feel like you are living a dream

This is what a King does for a Queen

Nothing will ever infiltrate that team!

what God truly put together

will last 50+ years withstanding any weather!

They will pray with and for each other

once they touch there will never be another lover

the Queen will always be loyal to her King

and he will always and forever make her heart sing

Their union will be a dream come true

This is what happens when you wait for what God has for you!

EIGHTH POEM

When it rains it pours

Love is an open sore

It's happy like football when a touchdown is scored

It's also angry like a woman scorned

When it rains we all get

Happy like a woman, when she's wet

Playful like a puppy being claimed as a pet

Scared as that puppy at the vet

When it rains from your eyes

You wonder simply "WHY"

Why is the sun not shining

Why are you on your knees whining

What is LOVE all about

Why does love make you scream and shout

When it rains it pours

I still stand in it, begging for more

Is it the sweetness or the pain, I want to endure

Honestly, totally, truthfully.... I'm not sure!

I do know if it's better to have loved than to not

Due to the fact love always hits the spot

When it's summer and sunny we seek shade

When its winter snow angels are made

When it's fall the wind turns us around

when it's hot and it rains it simply cools us down

Still confused on why when it rains it pours

It same reason why love is so damn hard so I'll never be sure!

NINTH POEM

Close your eyes, what do you see?
In my dreams, it's you right next to me
I love the way you make me feel
I'm wondering how could it ever be real
are you just a figment of my imagination
your hands on my body, what a wonderful sensation
in my ear, I want to hear the sound of your voice
the tingle it sends through my body making me moist
just thinking of you makes me smile
wanting to feel you makes me go wild
holding the thought of you inside
now I know this feeling is why I cried!

Dreaming of you

TENTH POEM

Some people ask me... am I a writer, a poetess, or a mogul.
And I simply tell them I don't know .
Some days I feel like Maya Angelou,
others I feel like Edgar Allen Poe.....
Some days I feel like Sistah Souljah,
others I feel like Zane....
Sometimes I feel a little crazy, other days I feel totally insane....
one thing is for sure
the amount of time it took me to mature.....
My God has placed this crown on my head....
I promise to wear it proudly until I am dead!!!
weather I am here to grace your stage........
or having you reading one of my novels page to page.....
I was put here on a throne.......
I am going to sit here gracefully with all my greatness being shown...
One thing I know is that God doesn't make any mistakes.........
He will always separate the real from the fake.........
So am I a mogul, a writer, or a poetess.......
I don't know but I'm here and I'm blessed.......
I have a voice and I will be heard.........
I'm teaching lessons even if that sounds absurd.........
I am showing women how to be mothers and wives.........
I need them to understand that no matter what we go through
we must live our lives...
I'm showing young girls how to read....,,
because my God said it only takes one to plant the seed!!!!!
I am QueenAmina for those that don't know......
I am a Poetess, a writer, and a one-woman SHOW!!!!!'

ELEVENTH POEM

I was just laying in my bed
and I was just thinking of something that really needed to be said
the reason relationships don't work nowadays
because we think in different ways
woman think meet him
learn him
love him
and be loyal to only him
whereas though men think
without a blink
find a chick
to stick
and if her clit
is wit
it's
it's lit
now you do have those women
I won't pretend
they think just like a man
knocking off what she can
and you do have those good men
that want to be committed living without sin
However, it seems that good men
find bad women
and Queens can't find their Kings
or acquire their wedding rings
I mean I'm just one person

I can't say for certain
just something I was thinking about while I lay
how cats and dogs love to play
how opposites attract
and most men love hitting it from the back
how men that pay rent and bills and do great things end up
with a woman that only wants to cause him pain
how women that work, cook, and clean
ends up with a man that's never seen
when he is
he's mean and angry with the stank face with a cold empty embrace
I don't understand why this is on my mind
I've thought about it several times
I'm thinking about this as I lay in my bed and I swear that
this just must be said
don't look at the cover
don't just look for a lover
look for a partner for good and bad
the one that will be there even if you never have
what I mean to say is when you're looking for a mate don't just date
that will get you nowhere
I'm being sincere
look for the version of you
if you really want to say "I DO"
I'm just talking while laying in bed
a few things I felt needed to be said!

TWELFTH POEM

As I type these words
I say them to myself in my head
Sitting on the edge of my bed
I am walking in my purpose
Heading toward my destiny I can feel it all around us!
Feel the newness of life descending my way
This is my time to shine there is NO time for play
I am educated but don't speak like it
I was taught with manners but don't act like it
I was told to have respect but don't show it
I was punished and rebelled from it
I was beaten and grew tougher from it
I was told to shut up and grew louder because of it
I was abandoned and survived this shit
And if you're in my way then you deserve to get hit
I know
A blow for a blow
It's worth it as you continue to grow
I learned how to just flow
As I type these words
I say them to myself in my head
Sitting on the edge of my bed
I am walking in my purpose
Heading toward my destiny I can feel it all around us!!

THIRTEENTH POEM

Today is a day that Allah made
Sitting back looking slayed
Embracing what is and what will be
Clear in my thoughts, making sure to see all that I can see
Leading and trendsetting is not my thing
Uplifting and Enlightening has a better zing
Don't be afraid to walk in your true self
Love and family is more important than wealth
Making memories
Building families
Motivating each other
Stronger sisters and brothers
Supporting from the heart
Happiness off the charts
Because this is a day that Allah made
Life isn't all about getting paid
We need to educate
You need to participate
With these youngsters to illuminate
What will be their fate
If they don't get back into the books

Stop worrying about looks
Understand themselves more
Stop being modern-day whores
Grow mentally
Internally
Emotionally
And Spiritually
In order to get closer to the most high
The one we all answer to when we die
Not only is this a day that Allah made
This is also a day that Allah can fade

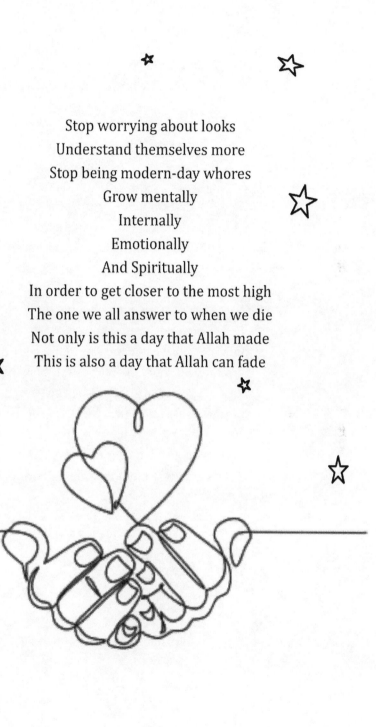

FOURTEEN POEM

Can you say for sure living without me would be good?
Or would you cry as hard as you could
If I was gone today or tomorrow
Would your eyes be full of sorrow?
Should you have yelled softer?
Could you have loved me harder?
Would you have answered my questions?

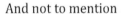

And not to mention

Should you have told me where you were going?
How do you think I felt never knowing?
Could you have just gone and got the pans?
Or did you always know that you weren't the right man?
Can you say that you did what I needed to be done
Or did you do what you wanted to like everyone
I am not your mom and I never want to be

But if you don't see
That this is a respect thing
Once you placed that ring
On my finger
It wasn't there to linger
You ask me and I tell
Anything I ask turns into a yell

A Scream

Always a nightmare never a dream
Is living without me good
Are you crying as hard as you could
Since you been gone all I see is tomorrow
No pain or any sorrow
I guess you should have yelled softer
Or maybe you could have loved me harder
Like showed mutual respect
Or gently kissed my neck
Either way
I am glad I live another day
without you
Bye Boo!!

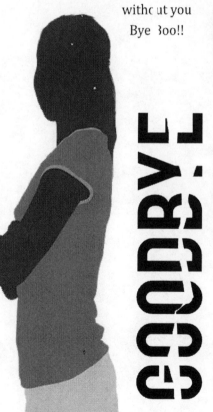

GOODBYE

FIFTEENTH POEM

When life gives you lemons
While running from demons
Trip and fall on your knees
Hold your hands together and beg God please

Please spare your life
Especially if you're living trife
Because when you're not right
Your movement ain't tight
Everything that you do will fall
No matter where you go no matter who you call
This is why I am telling you to live virtuous

Generous

Live your life with your hand open
blessing others while they're hoping
For better days
And sun rays
Because with lemons and rain
You're insane
If you think you made
Some lemonade

You still need some sugar to make it sweet
So help your fellow people so we can all eat!

SIXTEENTH POEM

I'm mad
I'm sad
I'm glad

I'm all the emotions to be had
All because you crossed the line
I was just fine
Not knowing your heart
Now we have to part
Can't even be friends
No way to make amends

All because you threw a monkey wrench in the plans
Acting like you were ready to be my man

Now look at us
Minus
No plus
No trust
Gone from my world
Really wanted to be your girl
I thought it would work
Instead I'm going berserk
All because you wanted to cross the line

For one good time
Tears
My fears
Damn dear
Did you not hear
Me say no
Then it was a go
Now you're a no show

Talking about getting all your ducks in a row
Now you've disappeared
Exactly what I feared

She is
STRONG
FIERCE
BRAVE
FULL OF FIRE

SEVENTEENTH POEM

Looking at my face you would swear I am the same
But I have grown a lot and I ain't got time for the game
If your plan
Is to be my man
Think again
That's not where to begin
I am of a very strong stature
Weakness is not in my nature
I will not sit and wait for you
So please do what you do
I make moves
Sway to my own grooves
My time is valuable
Your motives are questionable
I have grown and evolved
You are not my problem to solve
My name is Miss QueenAmina to you
Not, sorry, scrabble or clue
Looking at my face you would swear I am the same
I have grown a lot and I ain't got time for the games

EIGHTEENTH POEM

Why would you think that
you can mess with my mind
Neglect my behind
Talk shit, never kind
Sweetheart I truly don't have time
I am on a mission for perfection
It will need affection
My full attention
And all my motivation
Things that you cannot provide
While I am by your side
Down to ride
Smooth sailing my time to glide
I float above the peasants
I am heaven sent
No time for male infatuation
Now congratulations
Hope you learned a lesson
From all my confessions
I don't have time for the games
Fuck you lames
I'm not a girl in need
Not to beg and plead
for real intimacy
That's for me
Closeness
That's the best
Emotional support

Shall I abort
The conversation
Because my comprehension
Is an uncharted course
Because without remorse
I need you to understand
That in order to be my man
I will accept nothing less
Than the absolute best
A cut above the rest
Yes, I know I'm a mess
However I'm a rider
For my co-provider
My lover
My leader
My King
With or without a Ring

NINETEENTH POEM

Once in a lifetime
Love is finally mine
I've wanted you my entire life
Dreaming of being your wife
Loving you day and night
Solutions... never a fight
Waking up in your warm embrace
Going to sleep too your face
You are mine to have and to hold
Happy in love until we're gray and old

TWENTIETH POEM

Some people will waste your time and not give a fuck
Have you sitting around stuck
Snakes in the grass
Better watch your ass
Rats in the kitchen
Better make it your mission
To step off
Go get lost
Surround yourself
With like minded people
Find your equal

The ones that will celebrate your successes
Not set you up into big messes
That will lead you to better days
Educational objects and expensive ways

Not those bums
Grabbing for crumbs

Not the ones that want the food off of your plate
The ones who's demeanor is up for debate
They gotta go faster than fast
Grab a match and get the gas
Burn those ties
Because you're on the rise

Let's go team
It's not a dream
It is your choice
Let's hear your voice
Can you be your own person
Can you say for certain
That you're smart enough
Are you even tough
Do you have any street smarts
Are you creative in the arts
What can you contribute
Does that compute
Are you really that person wasting your own time
Think about that and not just because of this rhyme

TWENTY-FIRST POEM

When you live life to the fullest
Knowing you're meant to be the best
Above the rest
There is always a test
To see if you're a follower or a leader
A student or a teacher
A listener or a preacher
An enlightened seeker
Of better
down to the letter
I go hard for what I need
I won't crawl or beg or plead
I will continue to strive to be the best
I will pass every test
On my road I will also teach others
Fathers, sisters and brothers
and Mothers
to be just like me
Success is guaranteed
I strive not for riches or greed
but to see all people achieve
Their goals
take on positive roles
motivate the universe to change
the light is in range
We can all reach our stars
no matter how far
Just know that GOD is impressed
and he put us all here to pass a test!!!!!!!!!!!!!!

so never fucking rest
It's your job to be the BEST!!!!!!!!!!!!!!!!!

TWENTY-SECOND POEM

"I means need U"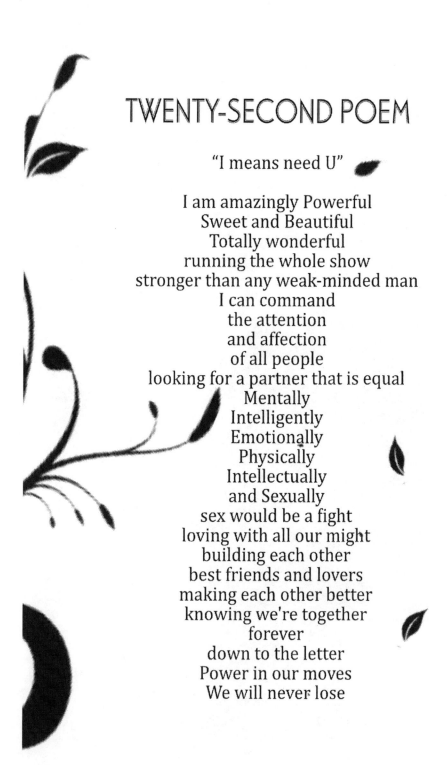

I am amazingly Powerful
Sweet and Beautiful
Totally wonderful
running the whole show
stronger than any weak-minded man
I can command
the attention
and affection
of all people
looking for a partner that is equal
Mentally
Intelligently
Emotionally
Physically
Intellectually
and Sexually
sex would be a fight
loving with all our might
building each other
best friends and lovers
making each other better
knowing we're together
forever
down to the letter
Power in our moves
We will never lose

stronger by the day
loving each other in every way
staying true to our mission
always hitting never missing
showing these people how it's done
Black Love will overcome!!!

TWENTY-THIRD POEM

A woman standing strong
working hard all day long
feet hurts between her toes
dust cloudy all in her nose
she keeps on trucking to make it through
She a woman what else can she do
Children to feed at home
She is a Queen on her throne
NO Kings by her side
just this strong woman and her pride
Teaching the children all she can
trying her best to make them understand
The world is a cold hard place
it is a battle, some kind of race
but never let it consume you
rise to every obstacle
embrace the pain as a lesson
look at each failure as a win
learn from within
is what a Queen teaches her children
After a long hard day
Of slaving away
working hard to make a better life for her kids
not worrying about how she lives
As long as her kids are strong
and don't end up having to work all day long
singing that sad ole song

her dreams are for her babies to belong
A Queen works hard her whole life
when she should be someone's wife
she makes the bread
then make sure her kids are feed
she hardly sleeps
complains not a peep
holds her emotions inside where they belong
because she a woman, and she MUST stand strong
Standing on her powerful feet she pushes off from her toes
And with every powerful moves she makes,
she exhales through her nose
Smiling all the while, "that's GOD" I suppose
As she continues to pollinate like a rose!

TWENTY-FOURTH POEM

You tried it
Like every other dick
Moving with the wrong head
Only thinking about the bed
Fuck what you said
Hate being mislead
But you tried it
Just wanted me to ride it
Shaking my damn head
I should lock you in a shed
Make it so several parts of you bleed
Oh shit I'm seeing red
All because you tried it
I could have denied it
But my heart dropped for you
You were part of the chosen few
That made me open my heart
Thought we'd never part
Thought you were a blessing
To my surprise you're just another lesson
You tried it and won
Pain is internally real... I'm done
You actually killed
What we built
You destroyed my joy
You selfish little boy

You thought it was a game
Causing destruction and pain
You played like it was a joke
Now I want to slit your throat
Because You tried It
But I won't take nobody's Shit!

TWENTY-FIFTH POEM

How trifling can you be
Stop returning shit to me
I don't want nothing from you
Go make it do what it do
You're an asshole
You didn't want to play your role
You're a lying motherfucker
A plain sucker
Men like you
Should be sued
You lie
Make woman cry
You think everything is a game
What a shame
I wish your mother never met your father
Why bother
You're a waste
Of space
You're what flies like
I'm glad you're now outta sight
Leave me alone
You're on your own
Remember you're grown
Drama prone
Can't tell the truth to save your life
So trife

I hate you and I never use that word
You're a fucking bird
I hope you get what you deserve from this earth
I see why none of your kids moms wanted you there at the birth
You ain't shit
Now you're dismissed

YOU'RE
DISMISSED

TWENTY-SIXTH POEM

Why would I love you
When you don't know how to be true
You are a liar and a cheat
I can't stand you all the way down to my feet
You always got a boogie in your nose
And your feet stink even between your toes
How did we go from I love you
To hate is your middle name
And you feel the same
What happens when you move to fast
Jumping in doesn't always last
Moving to quick
Now we hate each other shit
Sweet nothings
Are annoying
Not even something
Is now everything
Why would I love you
Were you ever true
Why did you lie
Make me cry
Why did you cheat
Another bitch on my seat
I did truly love you
You can lie to many but sweetie I'm a few
Wish I could rewind time
Never meeting you, with that I would be just fine!!

TWENTY-SEVENTH POEM

Hey Cutie
Who me beauty
I saw your face
Wanna walk your pace
Run your race
Get below the waist
What about my head
Yeah that too when we get to the bed
No I mean my brain
Are you insane
I wanna see what that ass do
What about STDs... AIDS, Gonorrhea to name a few
That's what condoms are for
Come get this stick that I got in store
What about crabs
You like these abs
What made you speak to me
Walk from A to B
These girls nowadays are fast
Don't take much to get that ass
Busting all down her throat
Then hand them they coat
Well Vagrant
I'm heaven sent
Can't just hit this booty
And don't call me cutie
I am the Queen
Woman of so many dreams
Just a kiss will make you scream

Totally natural no plots or schemes
I am as real as it get
Pussy's an ocean... fuck wet
Mental to impenetrable
I know what I'm capable
Of Love
Especially with GOD
So your messed up without me on your side
Kick rocks
With no shoes no socks
Out of my way
I'm on with my journey

TWENTY-EIGHTH POEM

I am so in love with me
With all that I am meant to be
You dimmed my flame
I almost forgot my name
They were still calling all the same
Even though I was ashamed
I let the Queen become gas
All because I believed your lying ass
I almost let the Queen fall
Knowing that for not only me do I need to stand tall
I am glad that I fell back in love with me
I have back my energy
I can fly
Kiss the sky
Travel the world
Become the right man's girl
One man's trash is another man's treasure
Trust my life is meant to be nothing but pleasure
I need Amina more than anything
And stop mumbling you can't sing
You destroying songs
Always wrong
I am so glad that I survived
I am glowing I'm so alive
I am standing on my own two
Way better without you
Happy on my ten toes
Ain't gotta watch you dig in your nose

Call hoes
Or fake pose
Damn I survived
Now I am on the rise!!!!

The Best In Urban Lit & Poetry!

Show-IT-Well Publications`

240-444-9029

aminashowell@showitwellbooks.webs.com

ORDER FORM

NAME OF BOOK	#OF BOOKS	PRICE OF BOOK	TOTAL
*ENTER THE MIND OF THE QUEEN (POETRY)		$15.00	
*THE QUEEN HAS SPOKEN (POETRY)		$15.00	
INNER SOUL (POETRY)		$15.00	
*IN THE HEART OF THE QUEEN (POETRY)		$15.00	
*QUEEN SURVIVED (POETRY)		$15.00	
*IF SOME WISHES CAME TRUE (NOVEL)		$19.99	
WISHES ACTUALITY (NOVEL)		$19.99	
*WHERE THE LOYALTY LYES #1 (NOVEL)		$19.99	
*WHERE THE LOYALTY LYES #2 (NOVEL)		$19.99	
*WHERE THE LOYALTY LYES #3 (NOVEL)		$19.99	
WILL'S DESTINYY (NOVEL)		$19.99	
*QUEENIE'S SECRET (NOVEL)		$19.99	
THE QUEEN PIN (NOVEL)		$19.99	
*Lessons Through Time (Novel by Madafah Lindsey)		$17.99	

Please note the following

Cash payments are strongly discouraged.

Payments for books can be made by PayPal, certified bank check or money order (please note that books paid for by personal checks must be cleared before shipment). Thank you for keeping Show-It-Well Publications in your thoughts and letting us fulfill your reading needs.

Sincerely,
Queen Amina
CEO Show-IT-Well Publications

COPYRIGHTS

Thank you to my Readers!

Made in the USA
Columbia, SC
11 August 2022

64590053R00045